Light

by Ellen Lawrence

Consultants:

Suzy Gazlay, MA
Recipient, Presidential Award for Excellence in Science Teaching

Kimberly Brenneman, PhD
National Institute for Early Education Research, Rutgers University, New Brunswick, New Jersey

BEARPORT PUBLISHING

New York, New York

Credits

Cover, © Moving Moment/Shutterstock, © XYZ/Shutterstock, and apdesign/Shutterstock; 2–3, © 3dimenti/Shutterstock, © CoraMax/Shutterstock, and © Designs Stock/Shutterstock; 4–5, © Serg64/Shutterstock; 4L, © 2xSamara.com/Shutterstock; 4R, © Monkey Business Images/Shutterstock; 5, © CoraMax/Shutterstock, © Mihai Simonia/Shutterstock, © Igor Kovalchuk/Shutterstock, © Alexander Ishchenko/Shutterstock, and © iStockphoto/Thinkstock; 6–7, © 3dimenti/Shutterstock and © CoraMax/Shutterstock; 7, © TonLammerts/Shutterstock; 8–9, © STILLFX/Shutterstock and © CoraMax/Shutterstock; 10, © Debra James/Shutterstock; 10–11, © CoraMax/Shutterstock and © TonLammerts/Shutterstock; 11, © Sergiy Kuzmin/Shutterstock and © Picsfive/Shutterstock; 12, © STILLFX/Shutterstock, © Sergiy Kuzmin/Shutterstock, © B.Calkins/Shutterstock, © John Henkel/Shutterstock, and © iStockphoto/Thinkstock; 12–13, © CoraMax/Shutterstock; 13, © TonLammerts/Shutterstock; 14, © Bilan 3D/Shutterstock, and © TonLammerts/Shutterstock; 14–15, © CoraMax/Shutterstock; 16, © Ilona Baha/Shutterstock and © Danny Smythe/Shutterstock; 16–17, © CoraMax/Shutterstock, © studiovin/Shutterstock, and © Piotr Krzeslak/Shutterstock; 17, © UpperCut Images/Superstock; 18, © Ivanagott/Shutterstock; 18–19, © CoraMax/Shutterstock; 19, © iStockphoto/Thinkstock; 20, © Debra James/Shutterstock; 20–21, © CoraMax/Shutterstock, © BelayaMedvedica/Shutterstock, and © STILL FX/Shutterstock; 21, © Piotr Krzeslak/Shutterstock and © UpperCut Images/Superstock; 22, © Samson Yury/Shutterstock, © Olinchuk/Shutterstock, © Igor Zh./Shutterstock, © Stefanovi/Shutterstock, © Anikanes/Shutterstock, © altanaka/Shutterstock, and © Capture Light/Shutterstock; 23TL, © chalabala/Shutterstock; 23BL © Ivanagott/Shutterstock; 23TR, © Fuse/Thinkstock; 23BL, © AJP/Shutterstock; 24, © Designs Stock/Shutterstock.

Publisher: Kenn Goin
Senior Editor: Joyce Tavolacci
Creative Director: Spencer Brinker
Design: Emma Randall
Photo Researcher: Ruby Tuesday Books Ltd.

Library of Congress Cataloging-in-Publication Data

Lawrence, Ellen, 1967– author.
  Light / by Ellen Lawrence ; consultants, Suzy Gazlay, MA recipient, Presidential Award for Excellence in Science Teaching, Kimberly Brenneman, PhD National Institute for Early Education Research, Rutgers University, New Brunswick, New Jersey.
    pages cm. — (FUN-damental experiments)
  Audience: Ages 6–9.
  Includes bibliographical references and index.
  ISBN 978-1-62724-093-2 (library binding) — ISBN 1-62724-093-4 (library binding)
  1. Light—Juvenile literature. 2. Light—Properties—Juvenile literature. I. Title. II. Series: Lawrence, Ellen, 1967– FUNdamental experiments.
  QC360.L39 2014
  535—dc23

                                        2013041494

For more information, write to Bearport Publishing Company, Inc., 45 West 21st Street, Suite 3B, New York, NY 10010. Printed in the United States of America.

10 9 8 7 6 5 4 3 2 1

Contents

Let's Investigate Light

On most days, you get dressed and go to school. In your classroom, you may read a book and do some math problems. Many of these activities would be really hard—and even impossible—without light. Light is a type of **energy** that lets us see the world. Inside this book are lots of fun experiments and cool facts about light. So grab a notebook, and let's start investigating!

Check It Out!

Light comes from different **sources**. The sun is our main source of light on Earth. It is a **natural** source of light. However, other sources of light, such as a lightbulb, are made by people.

Look at the pictures on this page.

▶ Which of the following are natural light sources and which sources are made by people?

(The answers are on page 24.)

flashlight

lightning

campfire

lamp

stars

5

How does light work?

Light travels from one place to another very fast. For example, light from a lightbulb travels throughout a room the instant a lamp is switched on. When the lamp's light hits objects in the room, the objects **reflect** the light. Because your eyes can see this reflected light, you are able to see all the objects in the room. Let's investigate!

You will need:

- A dark room
- This book
- A flashlight
- A notebook and pencil

1 When it's dark outside, go to a room in your home. Take this book, a flashlight, and your notebook and pencil.

2 Switch off all the lights in the room and shut the door. If there are any curtains or blinds, close them. Be careful not to trip over anything! Once the room is completely dark, try looking at this book.

3 Switch the lights back on. In your notebook, write down what happened.

▶ **What do you think you will see if you switch off all the lights but shine the flashlight on this book?**

Write down your **prediction** in your notebook.

4 Switch off all the lights again. Then shine the flashlight on the book.

▶ **What do you see?**

5 Switch the lights back on.

▶ **Does your prediction match what happened?**

Record in your notebook everything that happened.

▶ **When there was no light, could you see the book?**

▶ **Why do you think this is?**

▶ **What happened when you shined the flashlight on the book?**

▶ **What do you think was happening when the light from the flashlight hit the book?**

(To learn more about this investigation and find the answers to the questions, see pages 20–21.)

How does light travel?

When light travels from a light source, such as a flashlight, how does it travel? Does it move in a straight line or does it travel in other ways? Let's investigate what happens if something blocks the path of light.

You will need:

- A pencil
- A ruler
- Three pieces of cardboard, measuring 8 inches x 8 inches (20 cm x 20 cm)
- A pair of scissors
- Modeling clay
- A table pushed against a wall
- A flashlight
- A notebook

 Using a pencil and ruler, draw two diagonal lines on each piece of cardboard. The place where the lines meet is the center of each card.

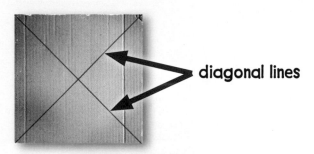

diagonal lines

 Draw a one-inch-wide (2.5 cm) circle in the center of each card. Ask an adult to help you cut out the circles.

 Stand each card upright using a lump of modeling clay.

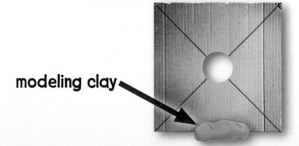

modeling clay

Place the cards on a table in front of a wall one behind the other about six inches (15 cm) apart. The holes in each card should be lined up so you can look through them and see the wall.

▶ If you shine your flashlight through the first card's hole, what do you think you will see on the wall?

Write your prediction in your notebook. Then use the flashlight to test your prediction.

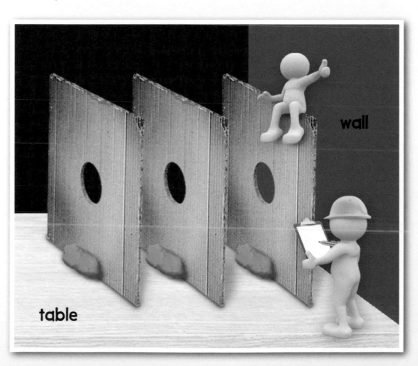

wall

table

 Now move the middle card to the right so that its hole is no longer lined up with the other two holes.

▶ What do you think will happen if you shine your flashlight through the first card's hole?

▶ What will you see on the wall?

Write down your prediction and then test it.

In your notebook, write down what you observed.

▶ What did you notice about the light when the holes were lined up?

▶ What happened to the light when the holes weren't lined up?

(To learn more about this investigation and find the answers to the questions, see pages 20–21.)

9

Which surfaces best reflect light?

In the first investigation, you discovered that objects reflect light. Do all surfaces reflect light in the same way? Let's investigate by shining a flashlight at different surfaces. You will need to carry out this investigation in a dark room with all the lights switched off and the door closed.

You will need:

- A dark room
- A mirror
- A flashlight
- A square piece of aluminum foil
- Poster putty or removable tape
- A notebook and pencil

1 Place a mirror on a table or other surface, or use a mirror that's attached to a wall.

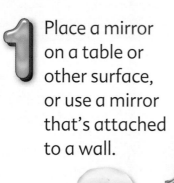

2 Switch off all the lights in the room. Stand slightly to one side of the mirror. Shine the flashlight into the mirror.

▶ **What do you observe in the mirror?**

3 Switch on the lights. Record in your notebook what you observed. Now attach the foil to the wall using poster putty or tape.

▶ **What do you think you will see if you shine the flashlight on the foil?**

Write your prediction in your notebook. Then switch off the lights and test it.

5 Now crumple up the foil and shine a flashlight on it.

▶ **What do you notice about the light?**

6 Finally, try shining the flashlight directly onto an area of the wall that has nothing on it.

4 Switch on the lights and record in your notebook everything you observed.

In your notebook, write down everything you observed.

▶ **Did the foil reflect light better or worse than the mirror?**

▶ **How about when the foil was crumpled?**

▶ **What did you observe when you shined the flashlight on the wall?**

(To learn more about this investigation and find the answers to the questions, see pages 20–21.)

Which materials can light shine through?

Light shines through some materials but not others. For example, light can shine through glass because glass is **transparent**, or see-through. Other materials let only a little light through. These materials are **translucent**. Some materials are **opaque** and block light. Let's try testing different materials to find out which ones light can shine through.

You will need:

- Different materials for testing (See some ideas in step 1.)
- A pair of scissors
- A notebook and pencil
- A flashlight

 Ask an adult to help you cut six-inch by six-inch (15 x 15 cm) squares from different materials.

cardboard

wax paper

colored tissue paper

aluminum foil

plastic bag

12

2 Look at each square of material.

▶ **Do you think light will shine through it?**

▶ **Do you think the material is transparent, translucent, or opaque?**

Write down your predictions in your notebook.

3 Switch off the lights. Hold up one of the squares about six inches (15 cm) from a wall. Shine the flashlight on the material.

▶ **Is the light shining through the square onto the wall?**

▶ **What can you see on the wall?**

▶ **Does the material let light through or does it block light?**

4 In your notebook, record everything you observe. Now do the same experiment with the other materials.

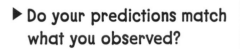

▶ **Do your predictions match what you observed?**

▶ **What do you think is happening to the light when it shines through a translucent material?**

▶ **What happens when it shines through something opaque?**

(To learn more about this investigation and find the answers to the questions, see pages 20–21.)

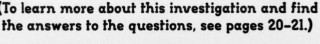

What happens when light is blocked?

Now you know that opaque objects block light. When light is blocked, a **shadow** is made. A shadow is a dark area where light cannot reach. Let's investigate shadows by making a funny shadow face!

You will need:

- Construction paper
- A pair of scissors
- Tape
- A popsicle stick
- A chair
- A plain wall
- A flashlight
- A notebook and pencil

1 Make a funny face using construction paper. Cut out the eyes, nose, and mouth using a pair of scissors. Tape a popsicle stick to the face to use as a handle.

2 Place a chair about four feet (1.2 m) from a wall. Turn on a flashlight and place it on the chair so it's pointing at the wall.

Switch off the lights in the room. Hold the face in the flashlight's beam about halfway between the wall and the flashlight.

▶ Describe what you see on the wall.

▶ What do you think has happened?

Switch the lights back on and write down your observations in your notebook.

▶ What do you think you will see on the wall if the face is closer to the flashlight?

▶ How about if it is farther away from the flashlight?

Write your predictions in your notebook. Switch off the lights again and test your predictions.

▶ Do your predictions match what you observed?

▶ Why do you think the size of the shadow changed?

(To learn more about this investigation and find the answers to the questions, see pages 20–21.)

15

What happens when light hits water?

Light travels through air in straight lines at very fast speeds. In fact, light can travel thousands of miles in just one second! When light hits water, however, it slows down. As light slows down, it bends, or changes direction. You can see this in action in this next investigation.

You will need:

- A glass with flat, smooth sides
- A jug of water
- A pencil
- A notebook and a pencil for writing

 Fill a glass halfway with water.

 Put a pencil into the glass of water.

3 Look at the glass of water from the top.

▶ **What does the pencil look like above and below the water?**

Record in your notebook what you see.

4 Now look at the top of the water through the side of the glass. Look at the pencil through the side of the glass, too.

▶ **What do you notice about the pencil?**

In your notebook, write down your observations.

Remember that as you looked at the pencil, your eyes were seeing light reflected from the pencil.

▶ **What do you think was happening to that light?**

(To learn more about this investigation and find the answers to the questions, see pages 20–21.)

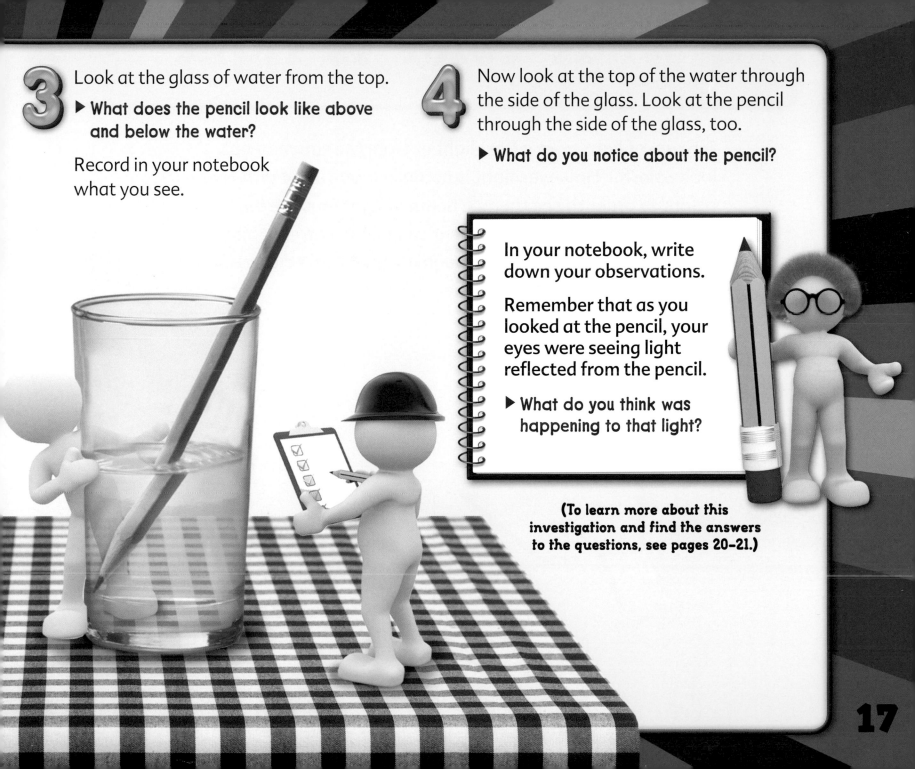

What color is light?

A beam of light from a flashlight or from the sun may not look colorful. However, light is actually made up of different colors. In order to see them, a beam of light must be bent. As it bends, it splits into different colors. We can see this happen when light shines through an object called a **prism**. It's possible to split light in other ways, too. Let's investigate!

You will need:

- A glass of water
- A sheet of paper
- A sunny window
- A notebook and pencil

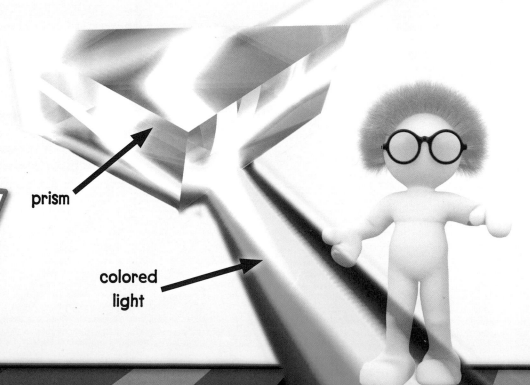

prism

colored light

1. On a sunny day, take a glass of water and a sheet of paper to a window where sunlight is shining through.

   ▶ **What do you think the sunlight will do if it hits the water in the glass?**

   Write your ideas in your notebook.

2. With one hand, hold the glass of water in the sunlight.

3. With the other hand, hold the paper beneath the glass. Position the paper so the sunlight passes through the glass of water and onto the paper.

   ▶ **What do you see on the paper?**

   ▶ **What do you think is happening to the sunlight?**

Record your observations in your notebook.

▶ **What colors did you see on the paper?**

▶ **Did the colored light remind you of anything?**

(To learn more about this investigation and find the answers to the questions, see pages 20–21.)

Discovery Time

It's fun to investigate light in our world. Now let's check out all the amazing things we've discovered.

How does light work?

If you couldn't see your book in the dark room, it was because there was no light reflecting off it.

Pages 6-7

When you shined the flashlight on the book, the book reflected the light. This made it possible for you to see the book.

How does light travel?

When the cards were lined up, the light from the flashlight traveled in a straight line through the three holes and made a circle of light on the wall.

Pages 8-9

Once the middle card was moved, however, it blocked the light from the flashlight. The light couldn't travel through the middle card or around it to reach the wall because light can only travel in straight lines.

Which surfaces best reflect light?

You saw an exact reflection of the flashlight's beam in the mirror because a mirror is shiny and flat and reflects light in straight lines.

Pages 10-11

Aluminum foil is not as shiny and flat as a mirror. It's good at reflecting light, but it can't make an exact reflection like a mirror. Crumpled foil is shiny but not flat. Its uneven surface reflects light in many directions so you see lots of bright sections of light on the foil.

A wall is neither shiny nor as flat as a mirror. A wall is not good at reflecting light. It scatters the light, creating a fuzzy glow.

Which materials can light shine through?

Transparent plastic lets light shine through it and onto the wall. Translucent materials, such as tissue paper and wax paper, let some light through. These materials scatter light, which makes the light faint and blurry on the wall. Opaque materials, such as cardboard, block light completely.

opaque

Now try looking at this book through each material. If you can see the book, it means light that is being reflected off the book is reaching your eyes through the material.

Pages 12-13

transparent

What happens when light is blocked?

The funny face blocked the light from the flashlight and made a shadow on the wall.

Pages 14-15

When you moved the face closer to the flashlight, it blocked more light so it made a bigger shadow. When you moved it farther away, it blocked less light so it made a smaller shadow.

What happens when light hits water?

When the pencil was put into the glass of water, the part of the pencil that was under water may have looked thicker. The pencil may also have looked broken or bent. Why did this happen?

Pages 16-17

When you hold a pencil and look at it, the light reflected by the pencil is traveling through air. However, when part of the pencil was put into water, the light it reflected slowed down and bent. This made the underwater part of the pencil look different than the part that was above water.

What color is light?

When the sunlight hit the water in the glass, it slowed down and bent. As it bent, the sunlight split into red, orange, yellow, green, blue, indigo, and violet light on the paper. These are the same seven colors you see in a rainbow.

Pages 18-19

21

Light in Your World

Now that you've made exciting discoveries about light, check out the ways you can see light in action every day!

1. Some things, such as the sun, are sources of light. Other things look very bright but are only reflecting light.

▶ **Which pictures show a source of light? Which things are reflecting light?**

lamp

disco ball

moon

headlights

2. The windows in your home are transparent and let light through.

▶ **How do you block light from coming in the windows?**

3. Stand outside on a sunny day. Look at the ground and you will see your shadow.

▶ **How is your body making a shadow?**

4. Sometimes, the sun shines when it is raining. Then you might see a rainbow in the sky.

▶ **What do you think causes a rainbow to form?**

Answers: 1. A lamp is a source of light. A disco ball reflects light. The moon reflects light from the sun. Headlights are a source of light. 2. Closing blinds, curtains, or shutters on windows blocks out the light. 3. Your body is blocking light from the sun and creating a shadow on the ground. 4. When sunlight hits raindrops, the water causes the light to bend. Then the light splits into seven different colors and makes a rainbow.

Science Words

energy (EN-ur-jee) power that can come from different sources; for example, light from the sun

natural (NACH-ur-uhl) something that is made by nature, not by people

opaque (oh-PAKE) not allowing light to pass through

prediction (pri-DIK-shuhn) a guess that something will happen in a certain way; predictions are often based on facts a person knows or something a person has observed

prism (PRIZ-uhm) a see-through glass or plastic object with flat sides

reflect (ri-FLEKT) when rays of light bounce off an object

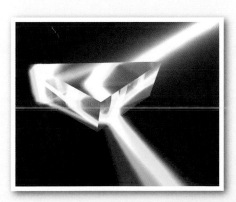

shadow (SHAD-oh) a dark shape made when something blocks light

sources (SORSS-iz) the places from which something comes

translucent (transs-LOO-suhnt) not completely clear; allowing only a little light to pass through

transparent (transs-PAIR-uhnt) completely clear; allowing light to pass through completely

23

Index

Read More

Ballard, Carol. *Exploring Light (How does Science Work?).* New York: Rosen (2008).

Nunn, Daniel. *Light (Why Living Things Need . . .).* Chicago: Heinemann (2012).

Nunn, Daniel. *Sources of Light.* Chicago: Heinemann (2013).

Learn More Online

To learn more about light, visit
www.bearportpublishing.com/FundamentalExperiments

About the Author

Ellen Lawrence lives in the United Kingdom. Her favorite books to write are those about nature and animals. In fact, the first book Ellen bought for herself, when she was six years old, was the story of a gorilla named Patty Cake that was born in New York's Central Park Zoo.

Answers for Page 5

- Lightning is a natural source of light.
- A flashlight is a source of light made by people.
- People build and light campfires, but fire is a natural source of light.
- A lamp is a source of light made by people.
- Stars are natural sources of light.